Little Mons You-Can-Make-It Book

by Mercer Mayer

to Fran Mitchell
who draws a mean monster

gb Golden Press • New York
Western Publishing Company, Inc.
Racine, Wisconsin

3. When you color the other monsters in this book, look at the
bulletin board if you want to use the colors Little Monster uses.

Professor Wormbog's Search for the Zipperump-a-zoo Game

Professor Wormbog, the famous monsterologist, has every beastie from A to Y in his Monster Zoo, but there is no beastie for the place marked Z. If he could only find a Zipperump-a-zoo, his monster collection would be complete.

Poor Professor Wormbog—he has searched high atop craggy peaks, far out on the restless blue sea, deep down in the caverns of the earth, but he can't find a Zipperump-a-zoo.

Now, you can help—play Search for the Zipperump-a-zoo and be the first in your neighborhood to catch a Zipperump-a-zoo for the professor. But look out! There are lots of tricky monsters lurking along the path to the Finish.

How to Put the Game Board Together

1. The game board is on pages 6 and 7. Tear out the pages and join them at the center. Make sure the paths line up across the center. Hold the pages together with a little tape at the top and bottom. Then turn the game board over and tape it together on the back.

2. The instructions for the game are on the back of the game board, so be sure to read them before you start playing.

Professor Wormbog's Search for the Zipperump-a-zoo Game

How to Play Professor Wormbog's Search for the Zipperump-a-zoo Game

You will need:
1. The game board—page 5 tells you how to put it together.
2. Different color buttons for markers.
3. Five pennies for telling the moves.

And no cheating!

Rules:
1. Each player chooses a button and puts it on START.

2. TO TELL WHO GOES FIRST, each player tosses the five pennies up, lets them fall, and counts the number that come up HEADS. The player who throws the most HEADS goes first and the play moves around the board from that player's left. If there is a tie in the number of HEADS, the tieing players toss again until the tie is broken.

3. TO MOVE, toss up the pennies and count the number that come up HEADS. Count off the same number of spaces on the board and put your button on the space where you finish counting. The pennies that come up TAILS don't count unless they *all* come up TAILS. If that happens, you get a special move of 6 spaces. If your move ends on a space with instructions in it, you must continue your turn by doing what the instructions say. If the instructions send you to another space with more instructions, you must follow those instructions, too.

4. FOLLOWING THE PATHS:
   a. Where the paths cross, you can go in any direction that the arrows point—but you can't go against an arrow.
   b. It's okay for more than one button to be on the same space at the same time.
   c. LOSE 1 TURN or WAIT 1 TURN. When you land on one of these spaces, you must wait while everyone else takes a turn. Then comes the turn that you have lost, so you wait for everyone else to take another turn. Then you can take your next turn.
   d. FREE TURN. When you land on one of these spaces, you get another turn right away, so you toss up the pennies and move again.

5. TO WIN, you must be the first player to get to the Zipperump-a-zoo in the FINISH space. As soon as you get to the FINISH you have won, even if you have some of your move left over.

6. SPECIAL RULES:
   a. JURFUS ISLAND. If you have thrown enough HEADS, you jump right out of the Jurfus' mouth and keep on going. If you stop in his mouth, follow the directions there.
   b. The CROONIE NEST and DOCTOR WINDBAG'S house each count as one space in the path.

Kerploppus Playing Cards

Tear out pages 9-16 and cut the cards out along the dotted lines. There are rules for games to play on pages 10 and 16.

9

Kerploppus Playing Cards

OLD WORMBOG,

a game for
two or more players

1. Take one Old Wormbog card out of the deck and set it aside. Deal all the rest of the cards to the players, one at a time. It's okay if some players have more cards than others.

2. Each player looks at his cards and picks out all the pairs, discarding them.

3. Each player then mixes up the cards left in his hand. The dealer starts the game by holding his cards out, face down, to the opponent on his left, who draws out one card.

4. If the drawn card makes a pair with a card in his hand, the opponent discards the pair. If the card doesn't make a pair, he keeps it in his hand. Then *he* mixes up *his* hand and holds it out face down to the player on *his* left, who draws out one card.

5. Play continues in the same way until all the pairs are matched up and discarded, and one player is left with the Old Wormbog card. That player is the Old Wormbog, and loses the game.

10

Murgatroy Norkley Olilifant Peevish

Quandrey Rankle Sqwerch Trollusk

Useless Verakisser Whizzle Xenostuwurst

Yalapappus Zipperump-a-zoo

Take a Break—

It's . . .

Snack Time! Old Wormbog

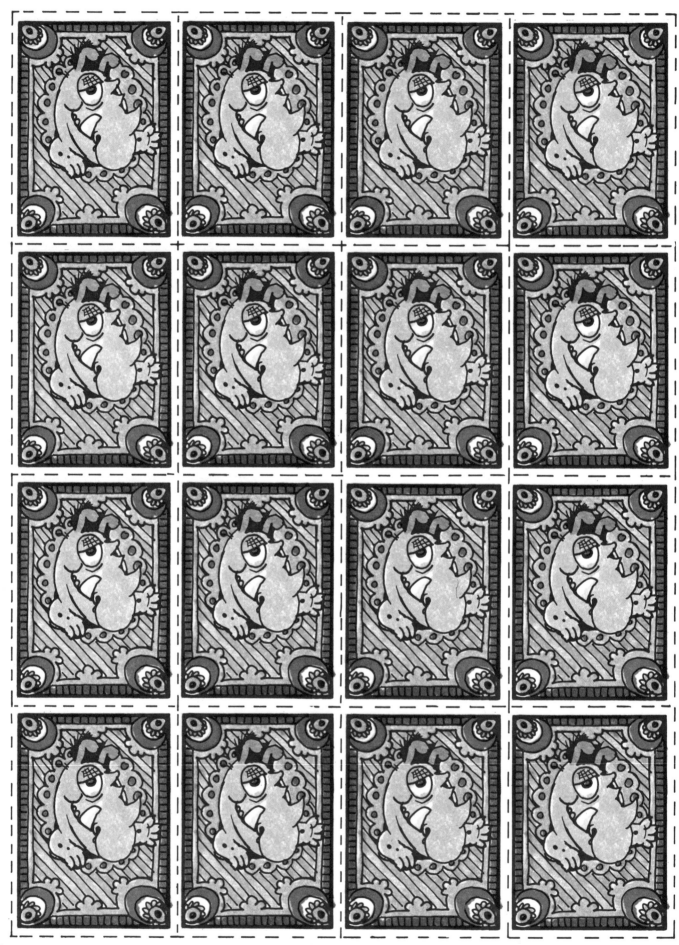

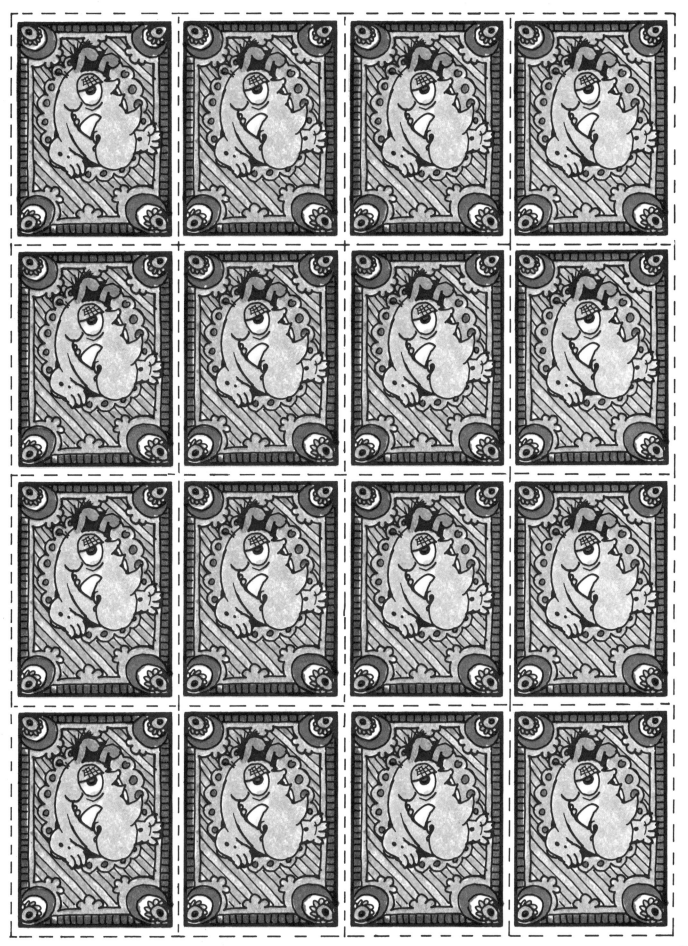

Murgatroy

Norkley

Olilifant

Peevish

Quandrey

Rankle

Sqwerch

Trollusk

Useless

Verakisser

Whizzle

Xenostuwurst

Yalapappus

Zipperump-a-zoo

Take a Break—

It's . . .

Snack Time!

Old Wormbog

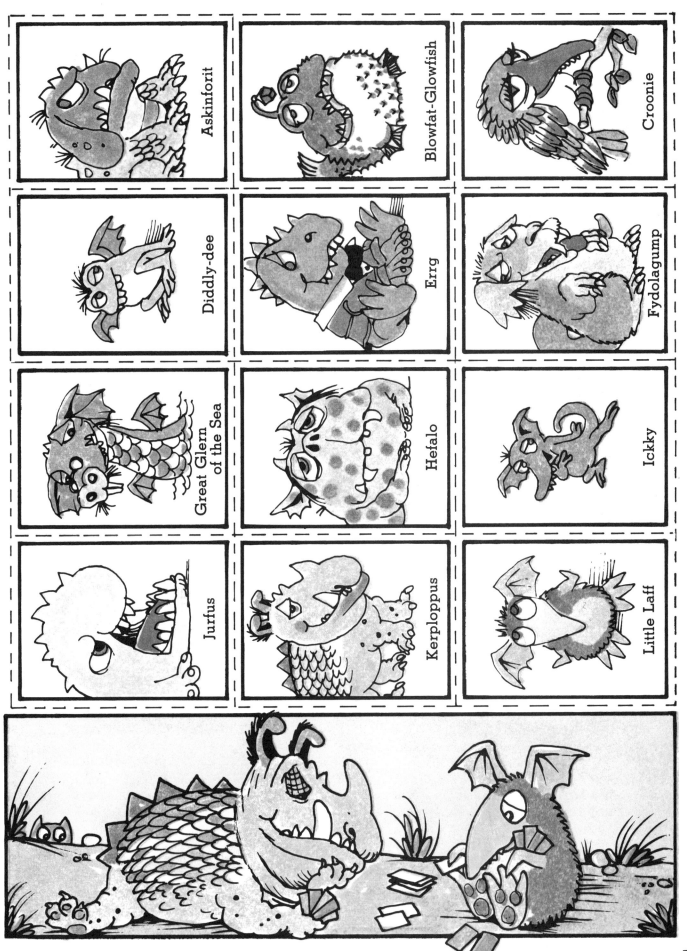

MONSTER MEMORY, a game for two or more players

1. Shuffle the cards and deal them all out face down on a table so that none of the cards touch each other. Don't try to get them in straight lines, just lay them out any way.

2. The beginning player turns two cards face up, one at a time, without moving either card away from its space on the table. If the two cards are a pair, the player takes them and puts them in his own pile of pairs won. Then he turns up two more cards. When he turns up two cards which are not a pair, he turns them face down again in their spaces on the table, and the turn goes to the next player.

3. All the players watch carefully, trying to remember the positions of the cards turned over, so they can find them later when they need to match a card.

4. The player who has the most pairs after all the cards have been matched up wins the game.

Monster Finger Puppets

1. Tear out the page and color the puppets.

2. Cut out each puppet along the dotted outline.

3. For each puppet, tape the ends of the base together so the base makes a ring that fits your finger. See the picture.

4. Have a play. You can make up a story—the sillier, the better!

5. Look on pages 19 and 20 to see how to make a little puppet theater with scenery.

Baby Brother

Little Laff

base

Little Monster

Big Sister

Useless Bl

Silly Thing

Trollusk

Little Glern of the Sea

Kerploppus

Zipperump -a-zoo

Sssnake

Professor Wormbog

Hi! Here I am,
your friendly Cut-Up.
I'm here to tell you to
turn to the other side of this
page to cut out the cutest little
MONSTER FINGER PUPPETS
you ever saw.

Monster Finger Puppet Scenery

Tear out the page and color the scenery.

Look on the back of this page to see how to make your stage.

Cut out along thick outline.

box-edge line

box-edge line

box-edge line

box-edge line

19

How to Make Your Monster Finger Puppet Stage

INSTRUCTIONS

A shoe box will be your little stage. (You will not need the lid.)

① Turn the box bottom up and draw two circles big enough to fit your hands through.

② Using a pencil, punch a hole through each circle.

③ Push scissors blade through each pencil hole and cut out circles.

④ Cut out trees from the front. Tape or glue an ice-cream stick to the back of each tree as shown.

⑤ Tape the trees to the inside of the front of the shoe-box stage, lining up the box-edge line with the top edge of the box. Be sure to check how it looks from the front.

back   back

box-edge line

box back

box bottom

⑥ Cut out the building scenery from the front, around the thick outline.

↑ JOIN LINE ↑

box front

(box-edge line)

⑦ Join the two pieces of building scenery at the join line. Match up the arrows and tape on the back. Tape or glue the buildings to the inside of the back of the stage. Line up the box-edge line with the top edge of the box.

⑦ To make the buildings stand up better, tape or glue ice-cream sticks to the back as shown.

JOIN LINE

box back

tape ← ice-cream stick

back

tape

stick

Here's how to hold the stage and puppets.

⑧ Paint or color the front and sides of your stage, or cover them with colored paper.

⑨ Your stage will look like this from the front.

JOIN LINE

Put on a show!

(Hands through the holes — thumbs stay under the box to support it.)

Turn the page over before you cut.

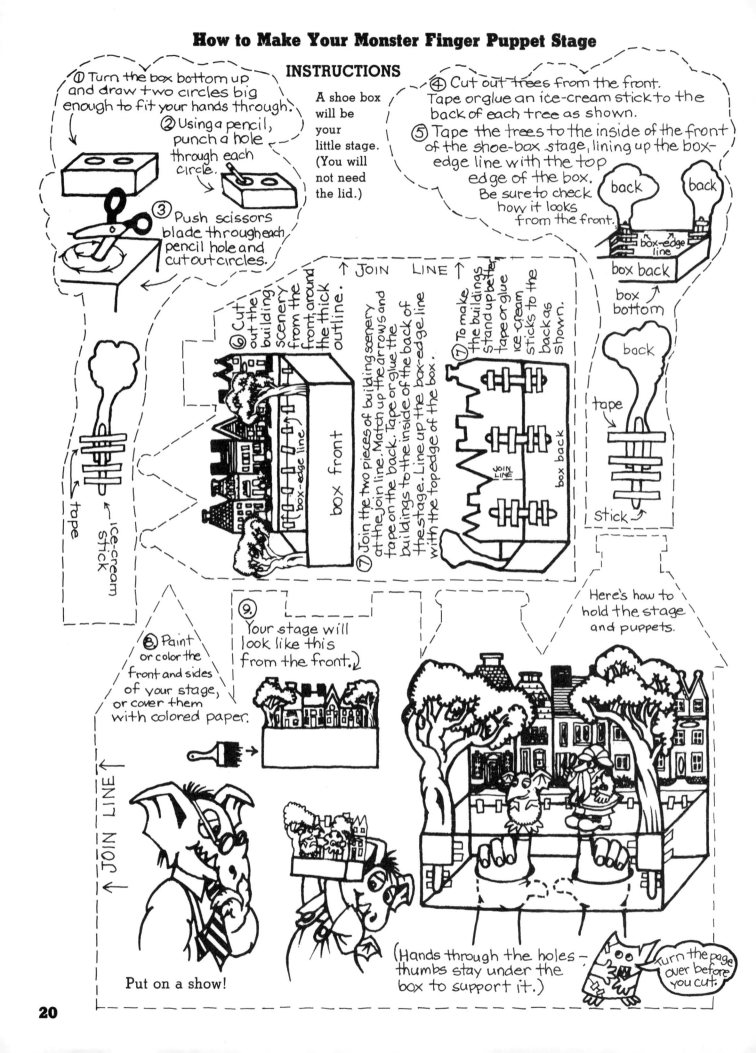

20

Monster Watches

Now, you can make it be any time you want it to be, with your own Monster Watches. Just wear the watch that tells the time you'd like it to be!

Turn the page to see how to make your Monster Watches.

watchband pattern

Monster Watches

How to Make Your Monster Watches

1. Tear out the page and color the watches.

2. Cut out the watchband pattern on the other side of the page. Lay the pattern on a sheet of colored paper and trace around it. Trace nine bands, in different colors if you like, one for each watch. Cut out the bands.

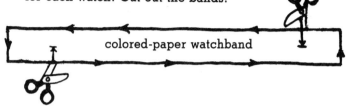

colored-paper watchband

3. Wrap one of the bands around your wrist and mark both ends at a spot where they overlap.

4. Cut a slot at each mark, cutting one slot down from the top of the band and the other slot up from the bottom. The slots will fit together as shown to hold the band on your wrist.

5. Use the slots on the finished band to mark where slots should be cut on the other bands.

6. Cut watches out along the solid outlines and glue or tape one to each band.

Well, here I am again, and just look at me. It's only page 22 and I'm cut up already! And that's only the beginning, because now I have to tell you to turn this page over and cut out the MONSTER WATCHES.

Little Monster and His Big Sister Paper Dolls

1. Tear out the pages and color the dolls, front and back. You will find Big Sister on page 27.

2. Turn the dolls face up and cut out along the solid outlines.

3. To make the dolls stand up, fold the stands and fasten as shown.

4. Color the clothes and then cut them out along the solid outline. Be careful not to cut off the tabs.

5. Dress Little Monster and Big Sister and make up a story about them.

Fold back.

Fold back.

Cut slots and fasten.

He's ready to go!

This is my back—turn me over to see my front.

stand

Fold back here.

Fold back here.

Cut

Cut

LITTLE MONSTER

Big Sister Paper Doll

BIG SISTER

Little Monster and His Big Sister Paper Dolls

Fold back.

Fold back.

Cut slots and fasten.

She's ready to go!

This is my back. Turn me over so I can see you.

stand

Cut.

Fold back here.

Fold back here.

Cut.

A Maze & Connect-the-Dots Puzzle

Somebody is hiding in Little Monster's secret tree. Help Little Monster and his friend climb through the tree maze to START and then connect the dots to see who's hiding there.

CLIMB HERE

Paper-Bag Puppets

1. There are two puppets. You will need a small paper bag for each one.

2. The puppets' faces and bodies are on pages 31-36.
   Tear out the pages and color them.

3. Follow the instructions on the pages to put your Paper-Bag Puppets together.

faces:
Cut out
along solid
outline.

backs of faces:
Turn them over
to cut them out.

back of body: Turn it over to cut it out.

Paper-Bag Puppets

How to Make Them

1. Tape or paste monster head on the bottom of the bag, as shown.

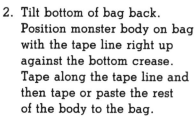

bottom of bag

2. Tilt bottom of bag back. Position monster body on bag with the tape line right up against the bottom crease. Tape along the tape line and then tape or paste the rest of the body to the bag.

bottom crease

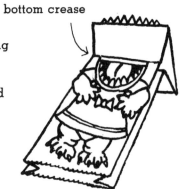

front of body: Cut out along solid outline.

tape line

Here's a finished
Paper-Bag Puppet,
ready to play with.

tape line →

front of body:
Cut out along
solid outline.

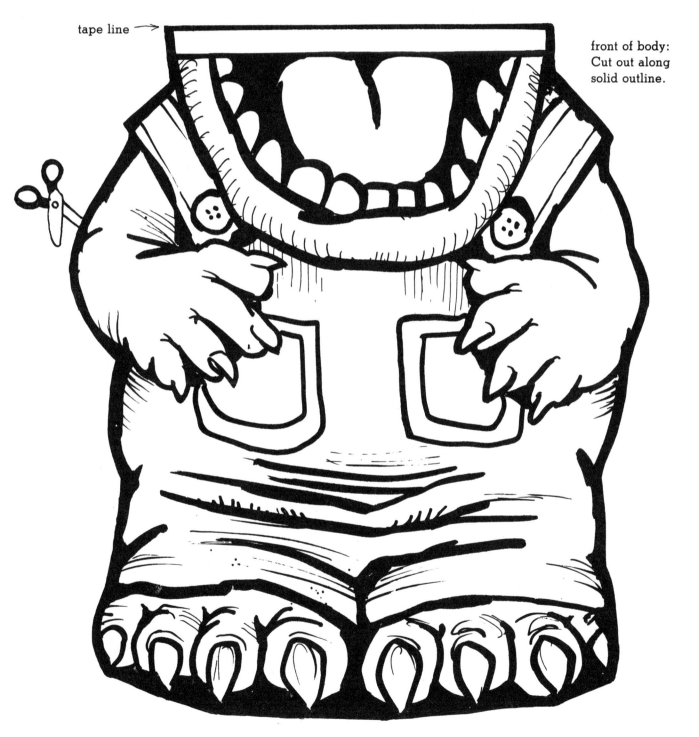

back of body:
Turn it over to
cut it out.

Trollusk Stamps

Look, another cut!
And that's nothing compared
to what'll happen to me
when you cut out the
TROLLUSK STAMPS on the
other side of this page.

YOUR
PICTURE
HERE!
Turn the page
to see what
to do.

How to Make Your Monster Picture Frame.

1. Tear out the page and color the frame.

2. Cut out around the outside of the frame. Follow the solid outline. Don't cut out the middle of the frame.

3. Paste your picture in the middle of the frame. Center it in the space.

4. Sign your name in the space below and give the picture to Mom, Dad, Grandma, Grandpa, or your friend for a present.

A PICTURE OF ME

To _____

From _____

Date _____

Monster Masks

string
hole

string
hole

#1 Sneedle

Look on the back of the mask
to see what to do.

1. Tear out the page and color the mask.
2. Cut the mask out from the front along the solid outline.

Sneedle Mask

3. EYEHOLES (Cut from the front):

a. Punch hole through each dotted circle with pencil point. (Keep fingers away from where point is going to punch through!)

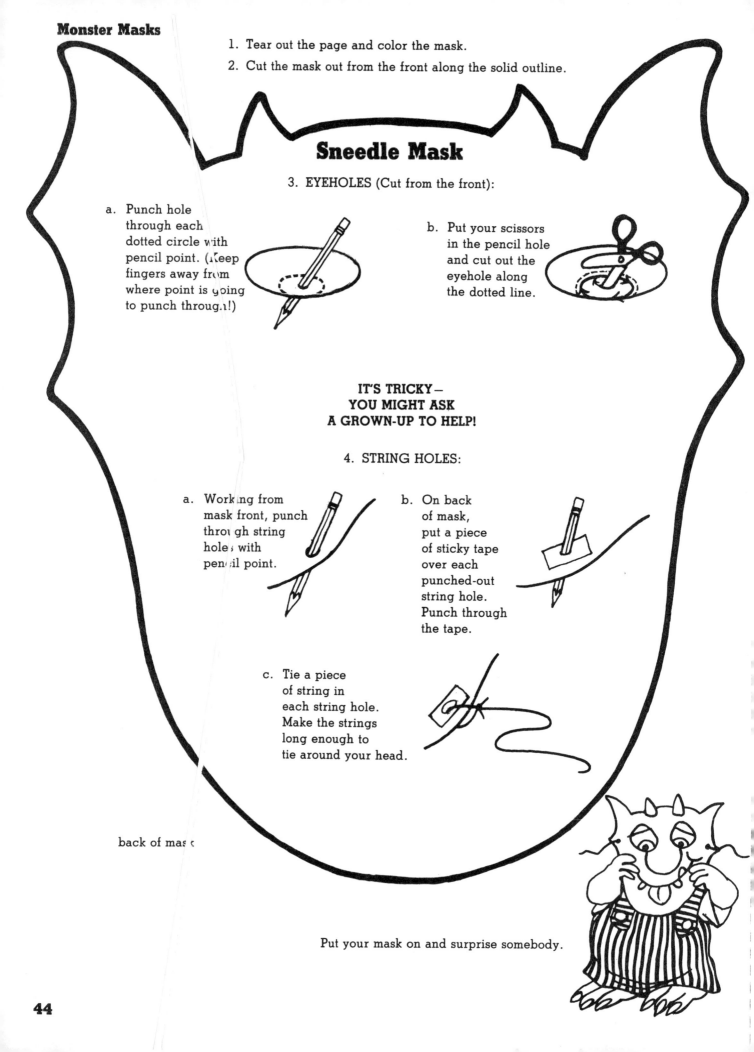

b. Put your scissors in the pencil hole and cut out the eyehole along the dotted line.

**IT'S TRICKY—
YOU MIGHT ASK
A GROWN-UP TO HELP!**

4. STRING HOLES:

a. Working from mask front, punch through string holes with pencil point.

b. On back of mask, put a piece of sticky tape over each punched-out string hole. Punch through the tape.

c. Tie a piece of string in each string hole. Make the strings long enough to tie around your head.

back of mask

Put your mask on and surprise somebody.

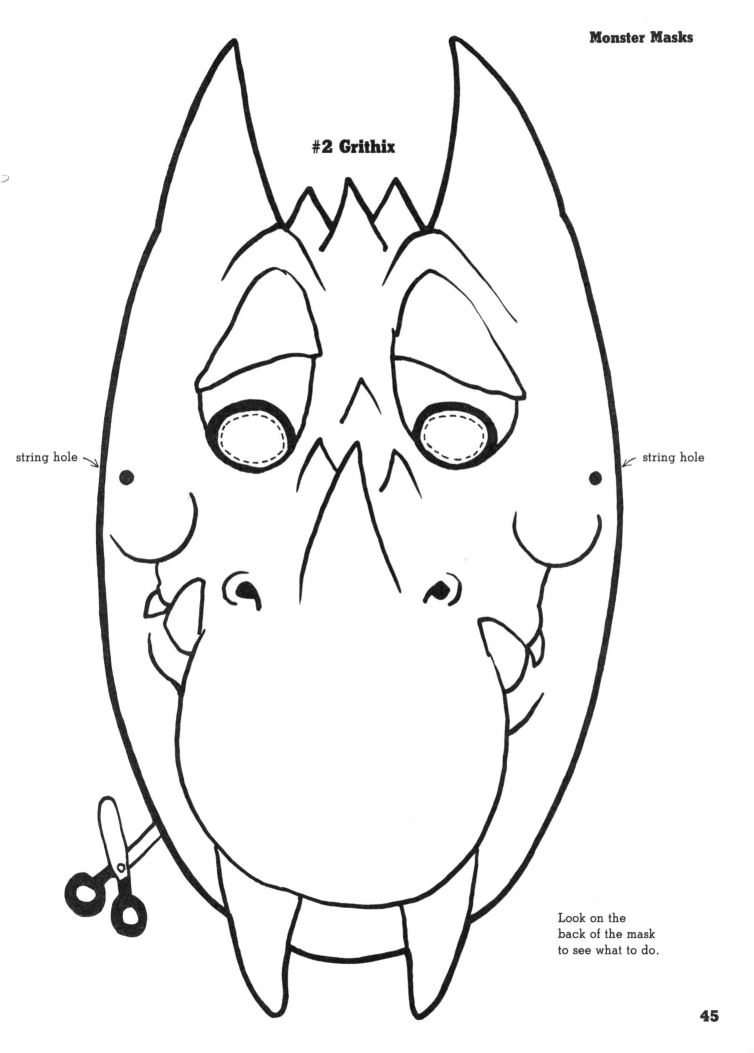

#2 Grithix

string hole

string hole

Look on the
back of the mask
to see what to do.

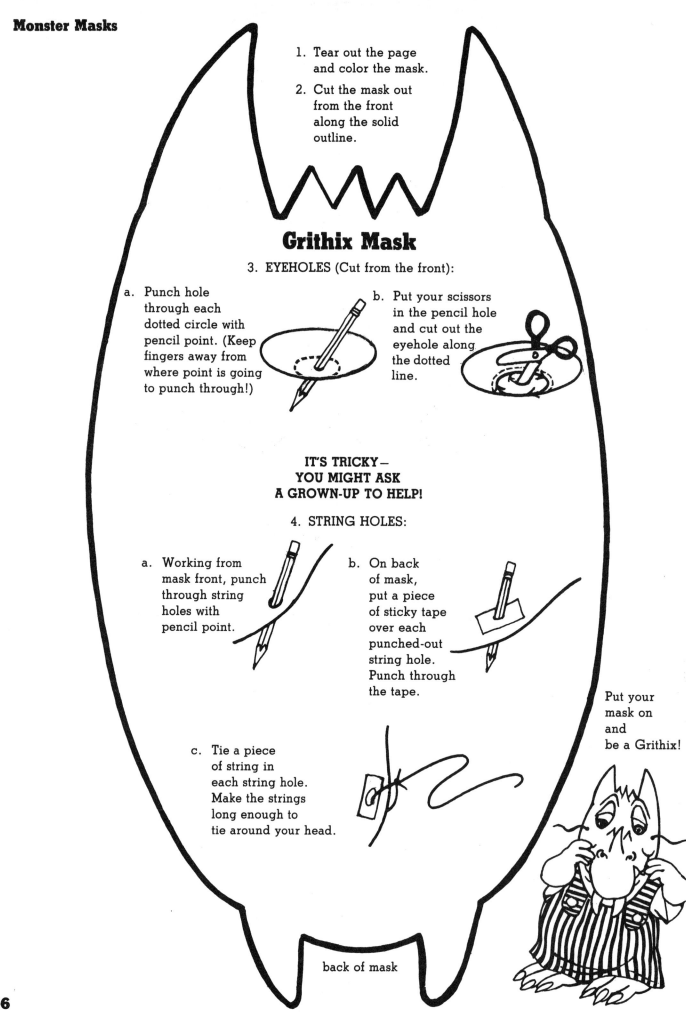

1. Tear out the page and color the mask.

2. Cut the mask out from the front along the solid outline.

Grithix Mask

3. EYEHOLES (Cut from the front):

a. Punch hole through each dotted circle with pencil point. (Keep fingers away from where point is going to punch through!)

b. Put your scissors in the pencil hole and cut out the eyehole along the dotted line.

**IT'S TRICKY—
YOU MIGHT ASK
A GROWN-UP TO HELP!**

4. STRING HOLES:

a. Working from mask front, punch through string holes with pencil point.

b. On back of mask, put a piece of sticky tape over each punched-out string hole. Punch through the tape.

c. Tie a piece of string in each string hole. Make the strings long enough to tie around your head.

Put your mask on and be a Grithix!

back of mask

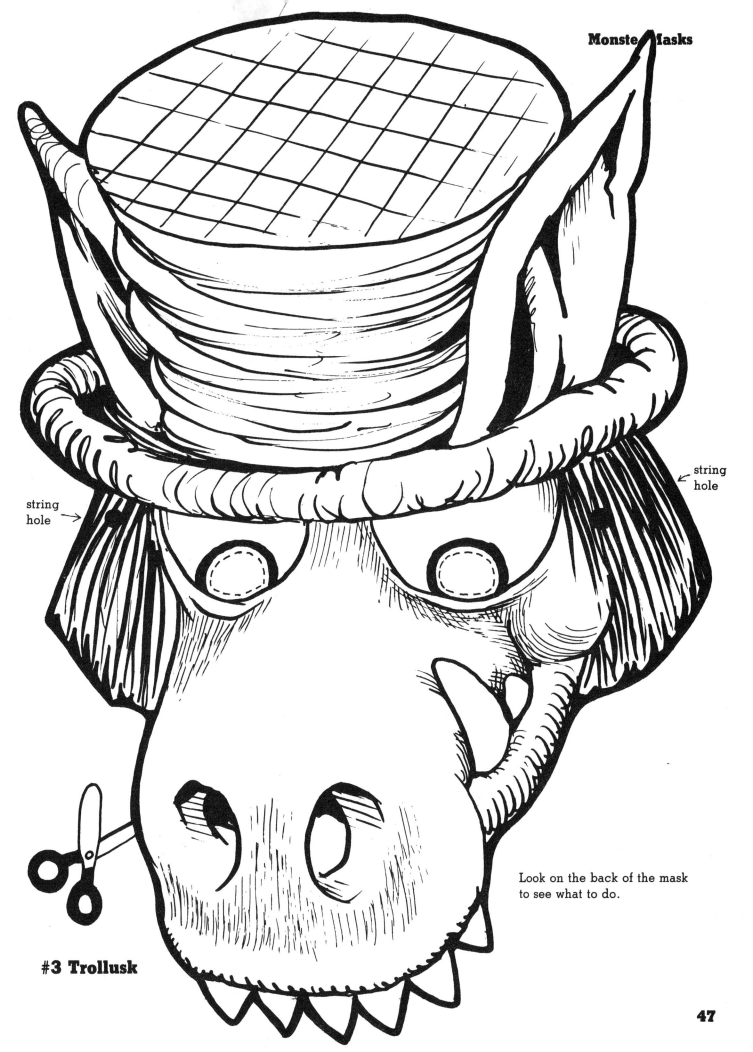

string hole

string hole

Look on the back of the mask to see what to do.

#3 Trollusk

Trollusk Mask

1. Tear out the page and color the mask.
2. Cut the mask out from the front along the solid outline.

3. EYEHOLES (Cut from the front):

a. Punch hole through each dotted circle with pencil point. (Keep fingers away from where point is going to punch through!)

b. Put your scissors in the pencil hole and cut out the eyehole along the dotted line.

IT'S TRICKY— YOU MIGHT ASK A GROWN-UP TO HELP!

4. STRING HOLES:

a. Working from mask front, punch through string holes with pencil point.

b. On back of mask, put a piece of sticky tape over each punched-out string hole. Punch through the tape.

c. Tie a piece of string in each string hole. Make the strings long enough to tie around your head.

Put on your mask and fool your parents!

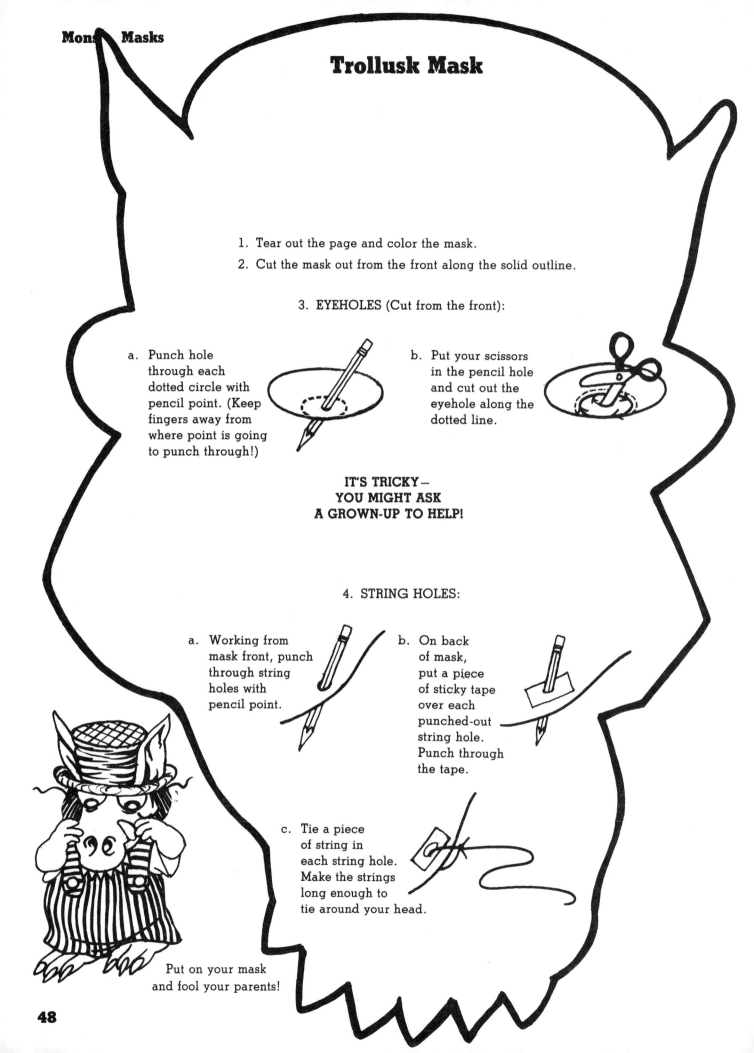

Flying
Bombanat
Glider

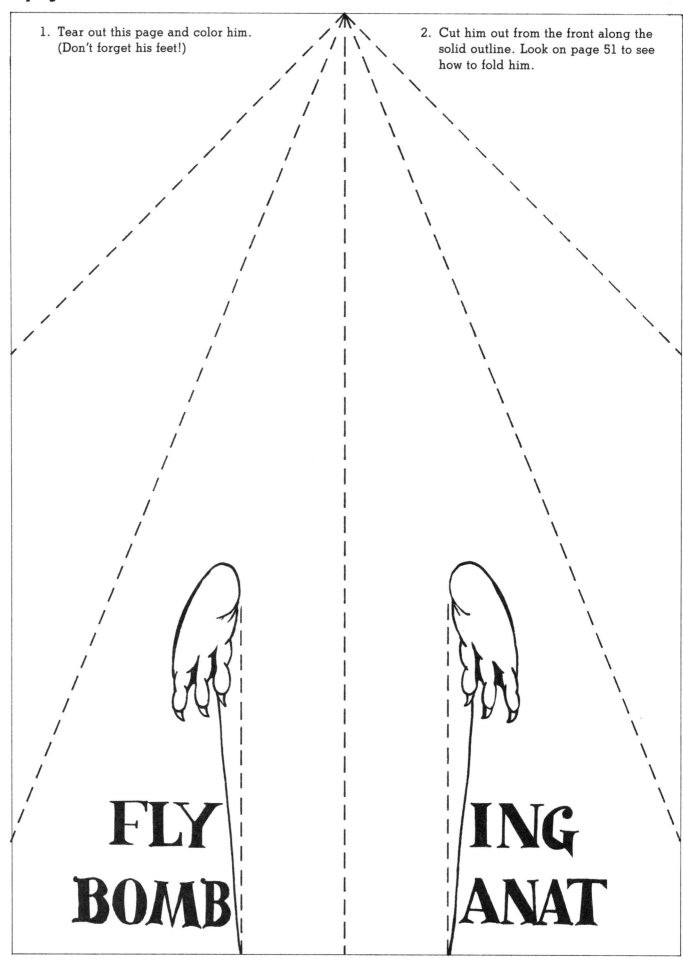

1. Tear out this page and color him.
   (Don't forget his feet!)

2. Cut him out from the front along the solid outline. Look on page 51 to see how to fold him.

FLY ING
BOMB ANAT

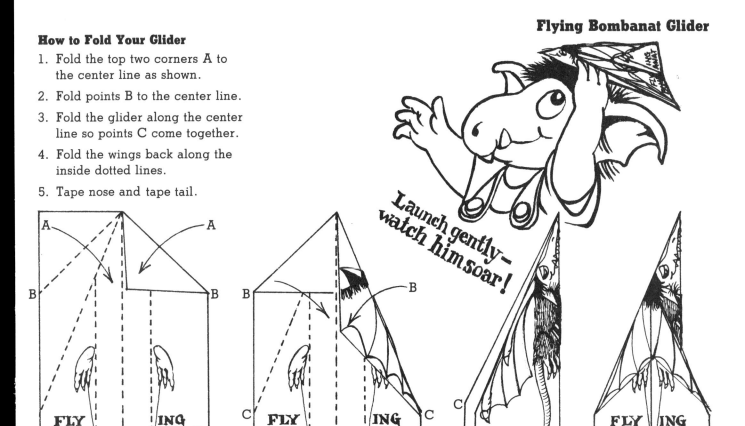

How to Fold Your Glider

1. Fold the top two corners A to the center line as shown.

2. Fold points B to the center line.

3. Fold the glider along the center line so points C come together.

4. Fold the wings back along the inside dotted lines.

5. Tape nose and tape tail.

Launch gently — watch him soar!

Bombanat Connect-the-Dots

Connect the Dots for a picture of a Bombanat in flight.

Doctor Windbag's Secret Code

Professor Wormbog's Kerploppus doesn't feel well. Find out what's the matter with him by decoding Doctor Windbag's medical message. Use the Secret Code Table below.

Doctor Windbag's Secret Code Table		
A ⇨	I ME	Q ⁄⁄⁄
B ⇦	J 🍉	R ⁘
C ⬇	K ◁	S ⊖
D 🐟	L ⇧	T ✳
E ▢	M www	U ⋀⋁⋀
F ◇	N >	V ⟋⟍
G 😺	O ⤨	W ♡
H ☆	P ⌃	X Y Z ⁘

Use this code to write your own secret messages!

What Doctor Windbag said: "He ate your hat and that's that!"

You-Can-Make-It Monster Face

You can design your own monster face.
Just use the blank monster head on the
back of this page, and the monster face
pieces on page 55.

When you have finished your monster,
tape it to the bathroom mirror so
Mom will get a surprise when she
combs her hair in the morning!

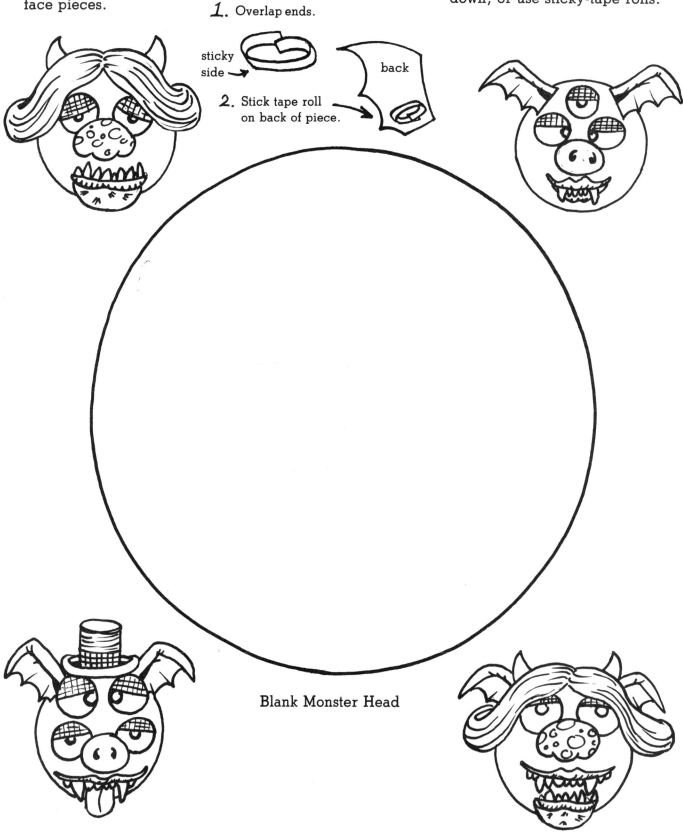

You-Can-Make-It Monster Face

What to Do

1. Tear out this page and cut out the blank monster head.

2. Tear out page 55 and color and cut out the monster face pieces.

3. Use the face pieces to design a monster face on the blank monster head. When you get a face you like, paste the pieces down, or use sticky-tape rolls.

Sticky-tape Rolls

1. Overlap ends.

sticky side →

back

2. Stick tape roll on back of piece.

Blank Monster Head

Monster
Face
Pieces

*Yikes—it's time to tell you
to turn the page over and
cut out the MONSTER FACE
pieces. I don't think I like this.*

Emilia Wingbat's Connect-the-Dots

Finish Emilia Wingbat's plane and color the picture.

Emilia Wingbat's Maze

Emilia Wingbat is lost in the clouds.
Be her navigator and show her the
way back to the hangar.
Then color the picture.

58

Turn the page to see what to do.

Tele-Monster-Vision (TMV)

Tele-Monster-Vision

How to Make Your Tele-Monster-Vision Set

1. Tear out the page and color the picture.

2. On the front of the TMV set there are two dotted lines, one at the top and one at the bottom of the screen. Carefully cut along those lines, making two slots. It will be easier if you first punch a little hole at the beginning of each dotted line with a pencil point. Then you can start the scissors in the hole.

3. Tear out page 61. Color and cut out the Tele-Monster-Vision strips.

4. To show a strip on your Tele-Monster-Vision set, thread it through the slots, from the bottom up, as shown.

5. Pull it up a frame at a time.

6. You can draw your own stories on the backs of the strips. You could tell a story about your birthday party, shopping with Mom or Dad, your best friend, your silliest mistake, anything you think is fun. Make a super-long story—tape the two strips together. Get more paper, and make more strips. Make a special holiday show for Thanksgiving or Christmas.

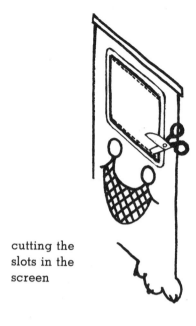

cutting the slots in the screen

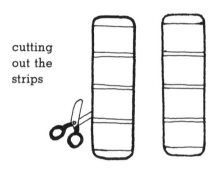

cutting out the strips

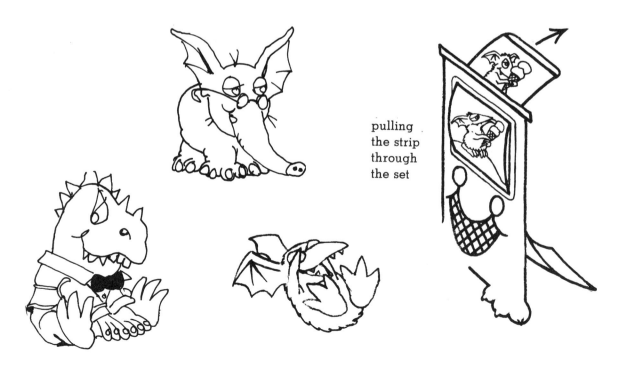

pulling the strip through the set

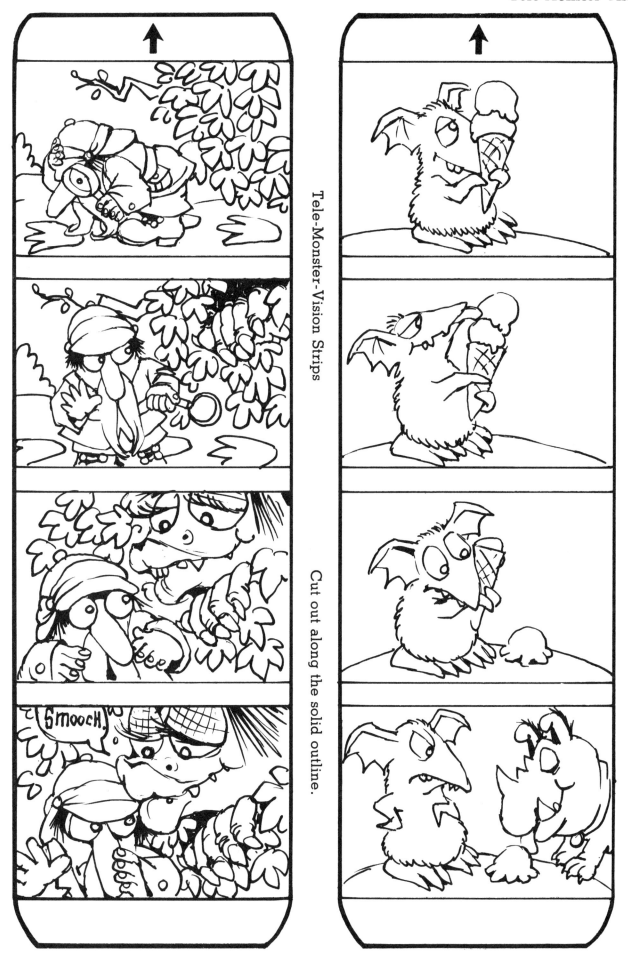

Tele-Monster-Vision Strips

Cut out along the solid outline.

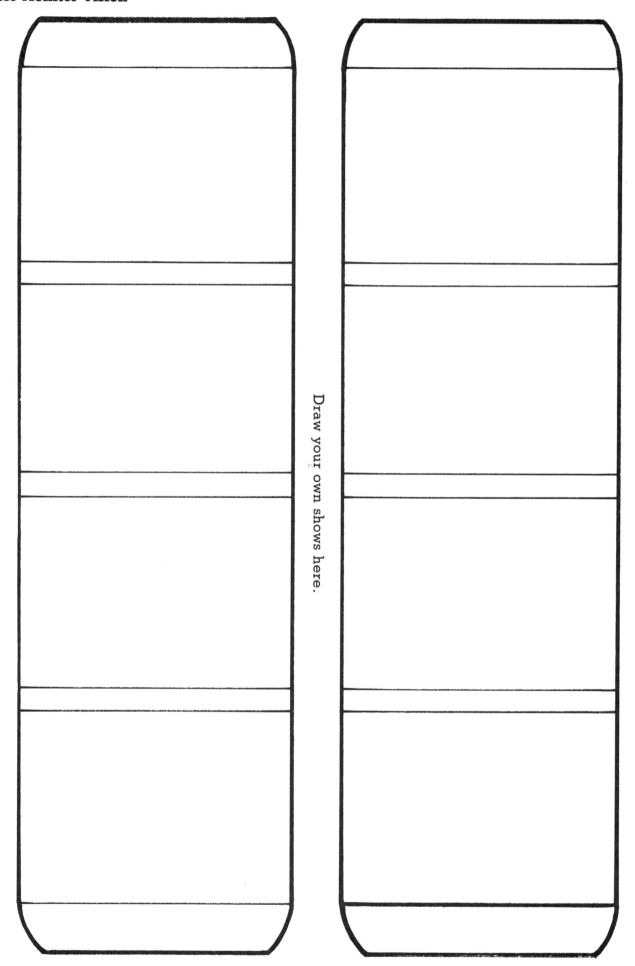

Draw your own shows here.

Feed the Paper-Munching Yalapappus
Paper-Toss Game

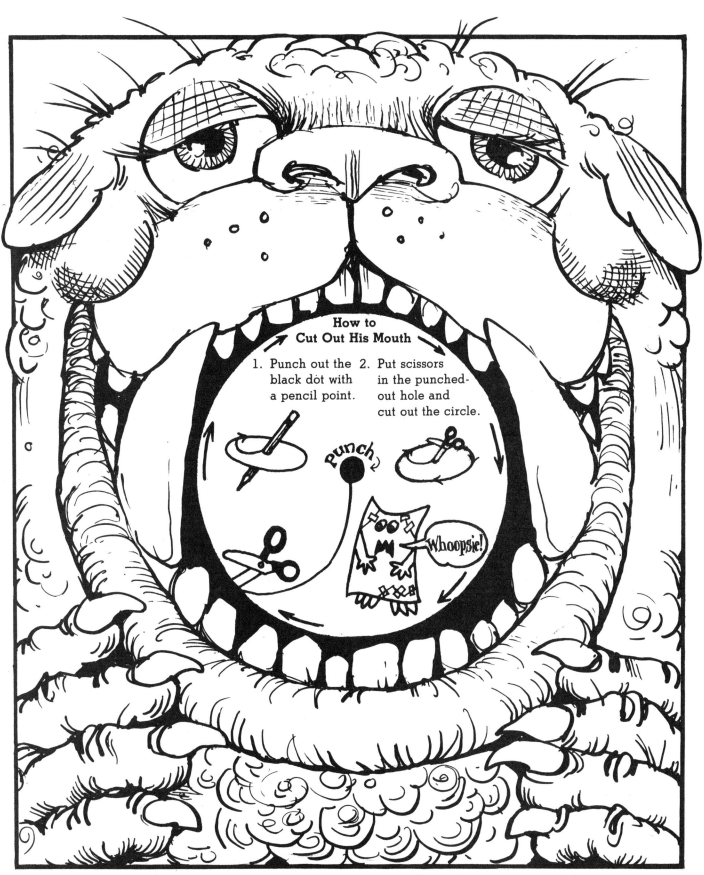

Feed the Paper-Munching Yalapappus Paper-Toss Game

How to Make the Game

1. Tear out the page and color the Yalapappus. Cut out his mouth as shown on the front.

2. Get a box with a bottom or side about the same size as the page.

3. Hold the Yalapappus against the box and draw around the inside of the mouth-hole so it shows on the box. Put the Yalapappus aside for a minute.

4. Cut the mouth-hole out of the box in the same way you cut it out of the Yalapappus. If the box is made of heavy cardboard, get a grown-up to help you cut it.

5. Tape the Yalapappus to the box so the two mouth-holes match.

About the Paper-Munching Yalapappus

The Yalapappus eats paper for lunch
And breakfast and dinner and snacktime and brunch.
Gaily he gobbles up yesterday's news
And merrily hums as his napkin he chews.

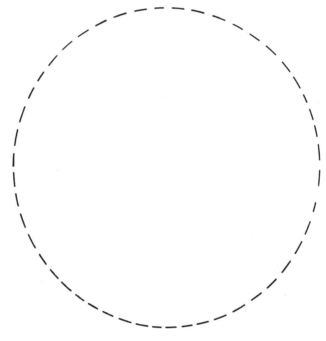

How to Play

Stand him up, wad up some scrap paper into balls, and try to throw them into his mouth. Hurry up, he's hungry! See how far away you can stand and still feed him. Take turns with a friend and see who can get the most in. For different flavors, get different color paper, or find some pictures of food in old magazines.

Yum!

Monster Signs for Your Room

Color these signs and cut them out. Tape them up where you need them.

Be sure not to tape them up where Mom *doesn't* need them.

OTHER WAY

SAVE THIS

YOU CAN'T FIND ME BECAUSE I'M HIDING

THAT WAY

BEWARE OF KERPLOPPUS

*Maybe if I stand way up
here at the top of the page
you'll miss me when you
cut out the MONSTER SIGNS
on the other side.*

More Monster Signs

Have fun with these signs in your room.

*Well, maybe if I stand
way over here at the
side of the page
you'll mss me when
you cut out the rest
of the MONSTER SIGNS.*

Monster Badges

Cut them out and wear them. Make a sticky-tape roll (see inside front cover) and put a badge on your shirt.

STAR

BE MY FRIEND

I QUIT

GOOD HELPER

TERRIFIC

YES INDEED

DO NOT SQUEEZE ME

BRAVE KIND HONEST GOOD SPORT

I HAVE 102 MEASLES

V. GOOD PROD

SUPER

FOLLOW ME →

KISS ME

CLEAN HANDS AWARD

FROM MUDSY TO SUDSY →

IT IS NEAT TO BE NEAT ★

69

*Help! No matter where
I stand, I always get
cut up. And now I'm
on the back of the
MONSTER BADGES.
I won't last long here.*

Monster Creepers

1. Tear out the page and color the creepers.

2. Cut out the creepers.

3. Curl each creeper by wrapping it around a glass—it should be curly enough to stand on its ends like the ones in the picture.

4. Make it creep across the floor by blowing on its tail.

Have a creeper race!

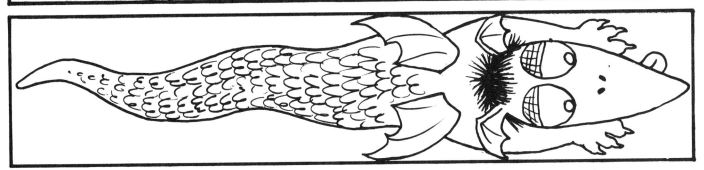

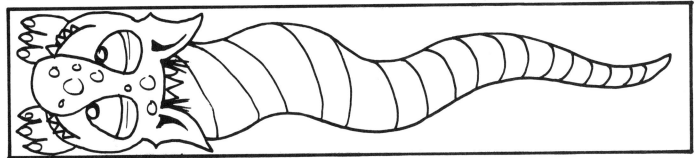

Aha. I've found a safe place this time. Go ahead and cut out the MONSTER CREEPERS on the other side of this page. Wheee—that was close!

MONSTER COMICS
TO MAKE YOURSELF.

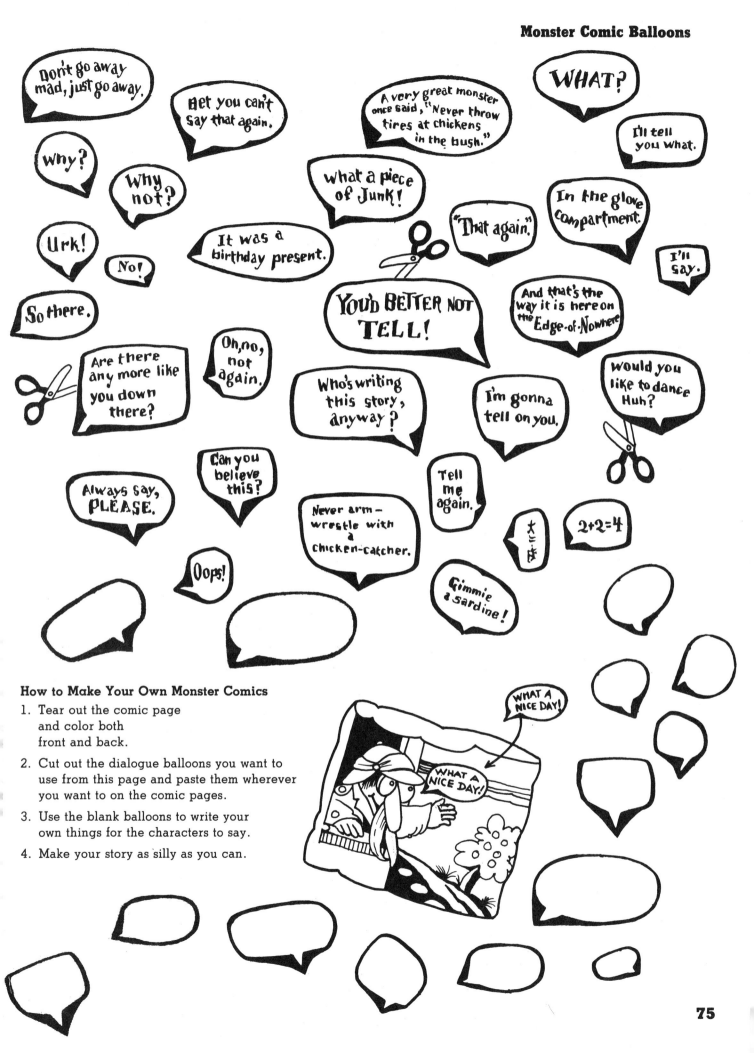

How to Make Your Own Monster Comics

1. Tear out the comic page
   and color both
   front and back.

2. Cut out the dialogue balloons you want to
   use from this page and paste them wherever
   you want to on the comic pages.

3. Use the blank balloons to write your
   own things for the characters to say.

4. Make your story as silly as you can.

*I wish I didn't have to
tell you this, but you're
supposed to turn the page
over and cut out the
MONSTER COMIC BALLOONS.
There's no place for me to
hide this time. Here I go again.*

Monster Puzzle

1. Tear out the page and color the picture.

2. Cut out all the pieces along the solid lines. If you want to, you can paste the page onto a piece of cardboard before you cut out the pieces. It will make them stiffer and easier to handle.

3. Mix up the pieces.

4. Try to put them back together. Good luck!

5. Keep the pieces in an envelope. Let a friend try to put the puzzle together.

*Now I'm on the back
of the MONSTER PUZZLE.
You don't really want
to cut out the puzzle
pieces, do you?
You do? I was afraid
you'd say that.*

Silly Monster Money

Tear out the pages and color the money.
Cut the bills out along the dotted outlines.

Silly Monster Money

Put some Silly Monster Money in Mom's wallet.

Silly Monster Money

Give Dad an allowance. Open a Silly Monster Money Bank.

Silly Monster Money

You can even use your Silly Monster Money to pay the babysitter.

Window Monsters

Wouldn't you like to roll up your window shade someday and see monsters looking in? Well, now you can. Turn the page to see how.

Window Monsters

How to Make Your Window Monsters

1. Tear out the page and color the monsters.

2. Cut the monsters out along the solid outlines.

3. Tape the monsters to the inside of your window against the frame so they look like they're peeking into your room. The picture shows how they will look.

4. Surprise somebody—put a monster in the window when they're not looking!

LET ME IN TO PLAY

How to Draw Little Monster

Follow the steps—draw lightly at first so you can erase the lines that you won't need later.

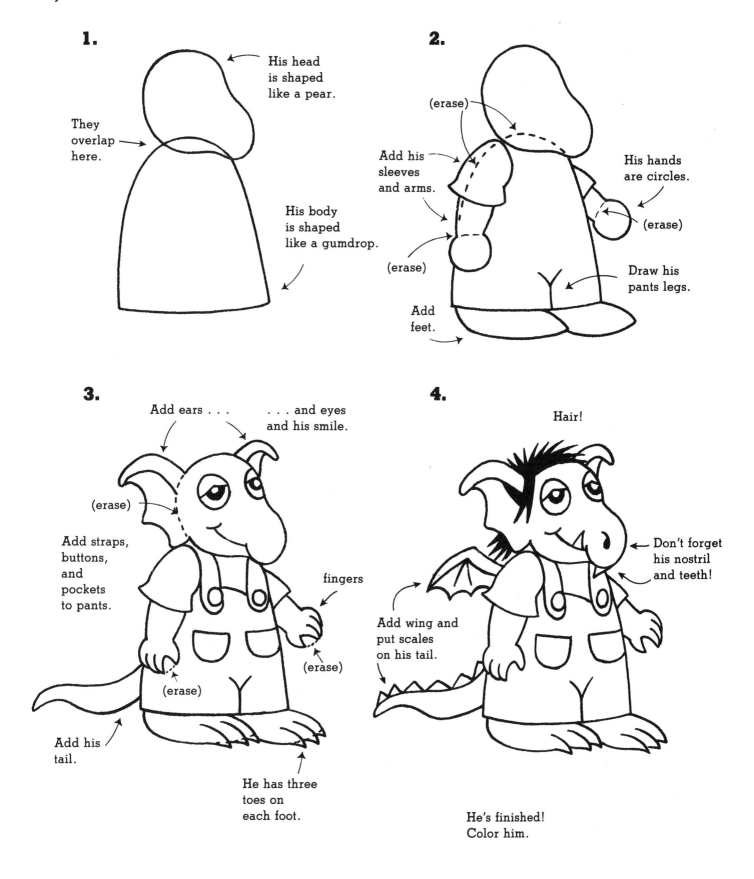

1.

His head is shaped like a pear.

They overlap here.

His body is shaped like a gumdrop.

2.

(erase)

Add his sleeves and arms.

His hands are circles.

(erase)

(erase)

Draw his pants legs.

Add feet.

3.

Add ears . . .   . . . and eyes and his smile.

(erase)

Add straps, buttons, and pockets to pants.

fingers

(erase)

(erase)

Add his tail.

He has three toes on each foot.

4.

Hair!

Don't forget his nostril and teeth!

Add wing and put scales on his tail.

He's finished! Color him.

The Great Glern of the Sea

Color Key

B = Blue   LB = Light Blue   G = Green   LG = Light Green

GY = Gray   OR = Orange   P = Pink

86   Follow this Color Key to color the Great Glern of the Sea.

Monster Spinner

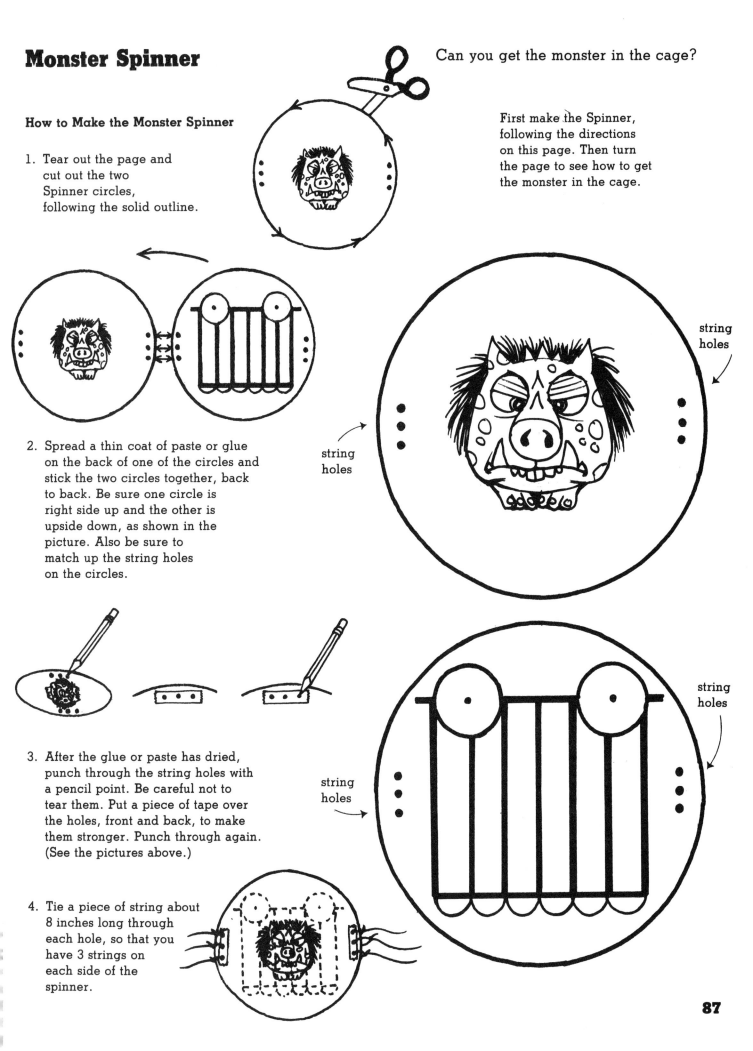

How to Make the Monster Spinner

1. Tear out the page and cut out the two Spinner circles, following the solid outline.

Can you get the monster in the cage?

First make the Spinner, following the directions on this page. Then turn the page to see how to get the monster in the cage.

2. Spread a thin coat of paste or glue on the back of one of the circles and stick the two circles together, back to back. Be sure one circle is right side up and the other is upside down, as shown in the picture. Also be sure to match up the string holes on the circles.

string holes

string holes

3. After the glue or paste has dried, punch through the string holes with a pencil point. Be careful not to tear them. Put a piece of tape over the holes, front and back, to make them stronger. Punch through again. (See the pictures above.)

string holes

string holes

string holes

4. Tie a piece of string about 8 inches long through each hole, so that you have 3 strings on each side of the spinner.

87

*Oh dear, you're getting
ready to cut out the
MONSTER SPINNER on the
other side of this page,
aren't you? Oh, I can't
look. Good-bye,
cruel world!*

How to Get the Monster in the Cage

1. Hold the ends of the strings in
   your hands as shown. Wind up
   the Spinner by twirling it
   around until the strings are
   all twisted around each other.

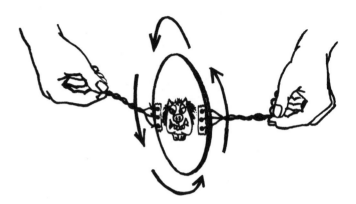

2. Make the Spinner unwind
   quickly by moving your hands
   apart, pulling the strings
   gently outward. Look at the
   spinning Spinner—the monster
   will appear to be in the cage!

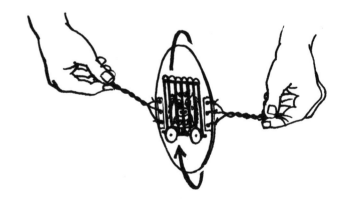

Monster Banger

1. Tear out the page and color the monster faces.
2. Cut out the Banger along the dotted outline.
3. Look on the back of these instructions to see how to fold the Banger.

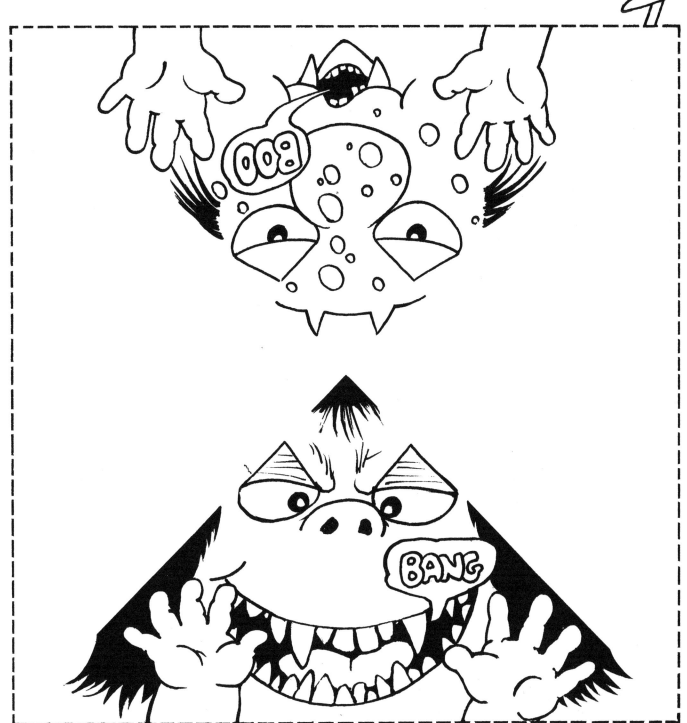

Monster Banger

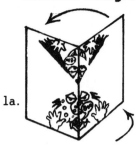

How to Fold the Banger

1a.

b.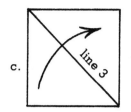

c.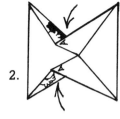

2.

1. Make three creases: a. Fold front halves together along line 1, crease and open.
   b. Fold back halves together along line 2, crease and open.
   c. Fold back halves together along line 3, crease and open.
2. Bring points A together, making the Banger fold into a triangle.
3. Hold the Banger as shown on the Banger side. To make it bang, raise your arm and bring the Banger down with a quick snapping motion.

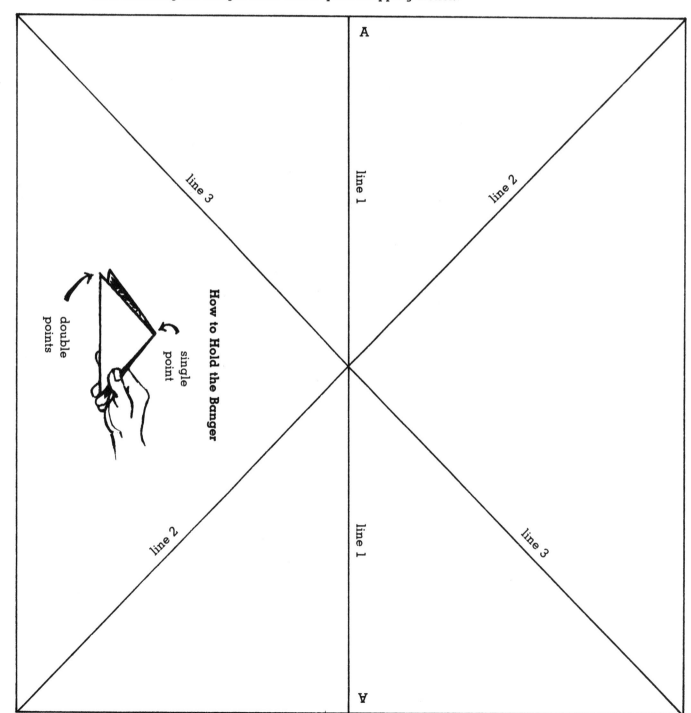

Little Biter

1. Tear out the page and color the Biter's face. (You may need to make him first to see how he looks, and then unfold him and color him.)

2. Cut out the Biter along the dotted outline.

3. Look on the back of these instructions to see how to fold the Biter.

Good for nibbling your friends!

HELP!

How to Fold the Biter

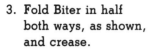

first fold

second fold

1. From the back, fold corners in to center along lines A, and crease.

2. Turn Biter over. Fold corners in to center along lines B, and crease.

3. Fold Biter in half both ways, as shown, and crease.

4. Hold Biter at points C and move your hands together so all four points C meet in the center.

5. Hold the points together where they meet and open out the bottom corners.

Look at Little Monster on the other side to see how to hold the Biter.

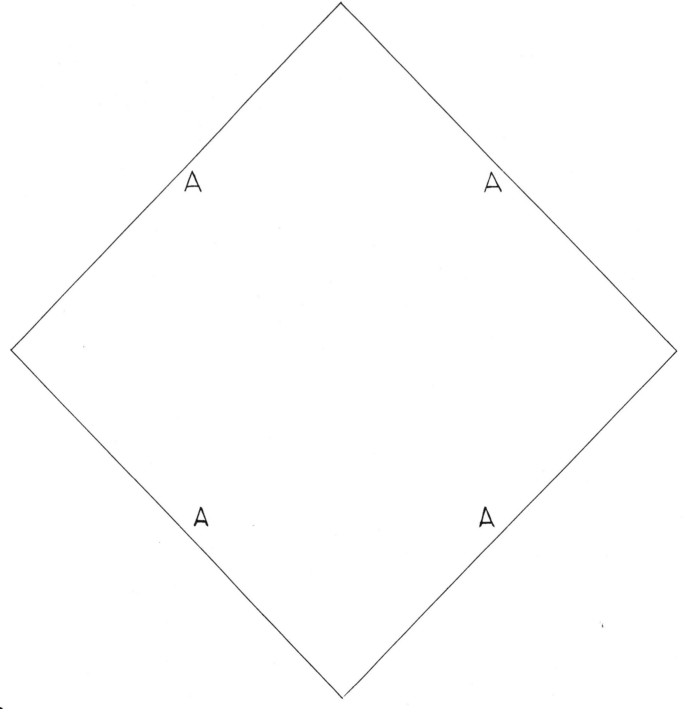

A   A

A   A

92

Professor Wormbog Paper Doll

1. Tear out the pages and color Professor Wormbog's front and back.

2. Turn him face up and cut him out along the solid outline.

3. To make him stand up, fold his stand and fasten as shown.

4. Color the clothes and then cut them out along the solid outlines. Be careful not to cut off the tabs.

5. Dress Professor Wormbog and make up a story about him. Take him to visit a friend. Let him play with your Little Monster and Big Sister paper dolls from pages 25 and 27.

Cut slots and fasten.

Fold back.

Fold back.

Quickly—turn me over, cut me out, and dress me—I'm cold.

Cut.

stand

Fold back here.

Fold back here.

Cut.

Professor
Wormbog

*Hmmph. Now I have to
stand on the back of a lot of
WORMBOG PAPER DOLL
clothes. Let me tell you,
a Cut-Up's life is
not an easy one.*

How to Make Your Reward Poster

1. Tear out the page and color the poster.

2. Cut out around the outside of the poster. Follow the solid outline. Don't cut out the middle of the poster.

3. Paste your picture (or the picture of the rascal in question) in the middle of the poster. Center it in the space.

4. Sign your name in the space below and give the picture to a relative or a friend. Or hang it in the Sheriff's Office when you play cowboys. It would probably also look nice hanging on the refrigerator.

A PICTURE OF_____

To _____

From _____

Date _____

Mix-A-Monsters

Look over here to see what to do. →

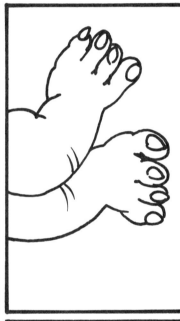

3. Make a monster by combining any head, middle, and feet. Make a monster with a head at both ends. Mix up the pieces and see who can make the funniest monster.

2. Cut out the heads, middles, and feet of the monsters along the solid outlines.

1. Tear out the page and color the monsters on both sides.

Mix-A-Monsters

Look on
the other
side of
the page
to see
what
to do.

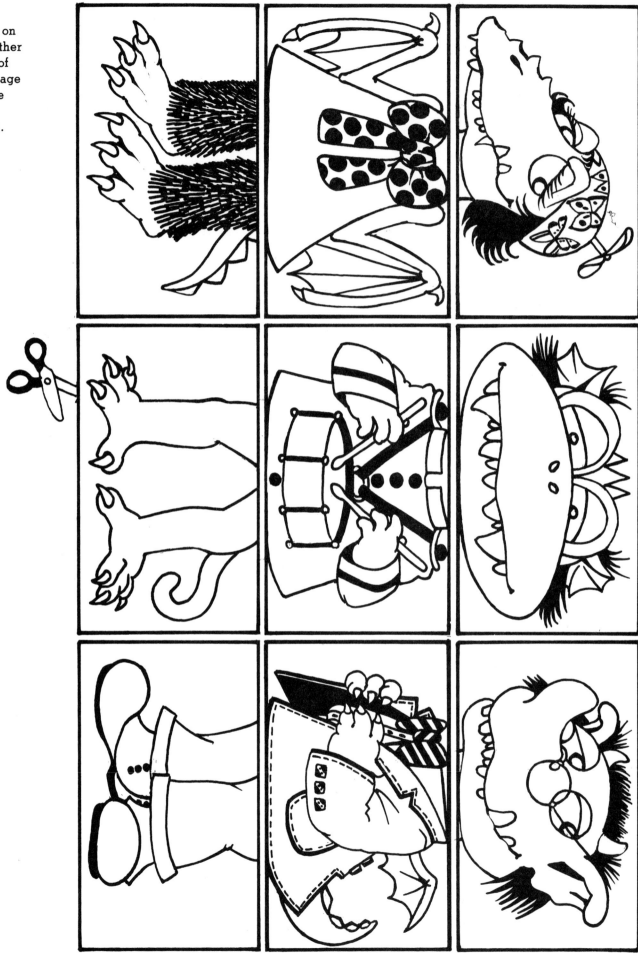

Turn the page to see what to do.

Pin the Tail on the Kerploppus

How to Make the Game

1. Tear out this page and the next one and color the Kerploppus and all the tails.

2. Cut out the tails and put a pushpin through the hole in the top of each one. If you don't have any pushpins, you might use a little piece of tape at the top of each tail.

3. Tape the Kerploppus up on a large carton or on the wall. If you put it on the wall, first tape it to a piece of thick cardboard for the pins to stick into. (If you are using tape on the tails then you won't need the thick cardboard.) Also, be sure to ask Mom or Dad to show you a wall that's okay to use.

How to Play Pin the Tail on the Kerploppus

1. Each player gets a tail.

2. Decide who goes first by flipping a coin, or by some other way you like.

3. Blindfold the first player with a handkerchief, turn him around a few times, then point him toward the Kerploppus.

4. The player tries to pin or tape the tail on the Kerploppus as close as possible to where it belongs (the center of the target).

5. After everyone has taken a turn, the person who got his or her tail the closest is the winner.

Tails

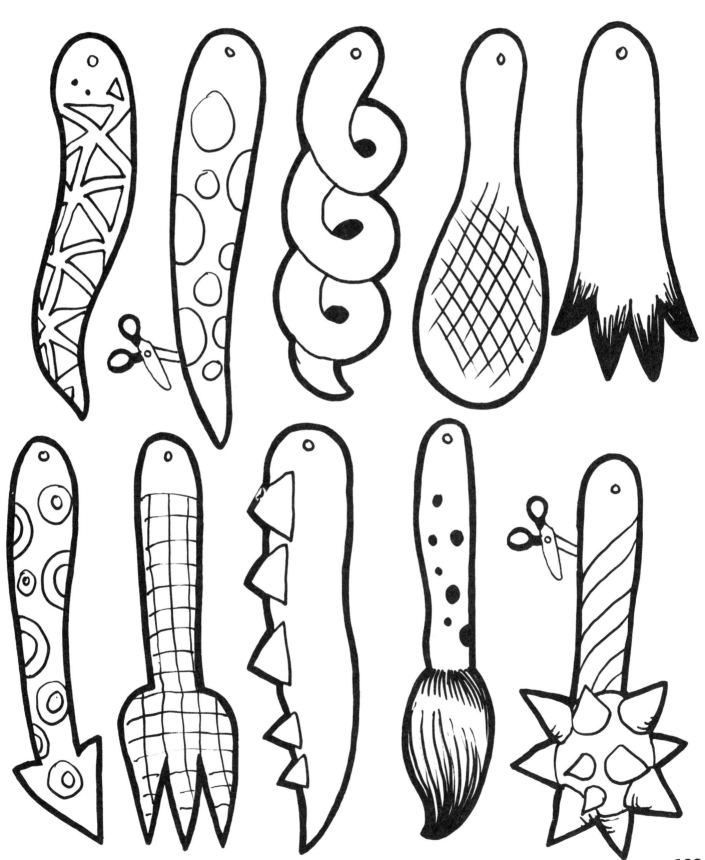

These are the backs of the tails.
Turn the page over to cut them out.

Monster Mobile

LETTER-EATING BOMBANAT

Tear out the page and color the monsters.

STAMP-COLLECTING TROLLUSK

Look on page 107 to see how to make the mobile.

PAPER-MUNCHING YALAPAPPUS

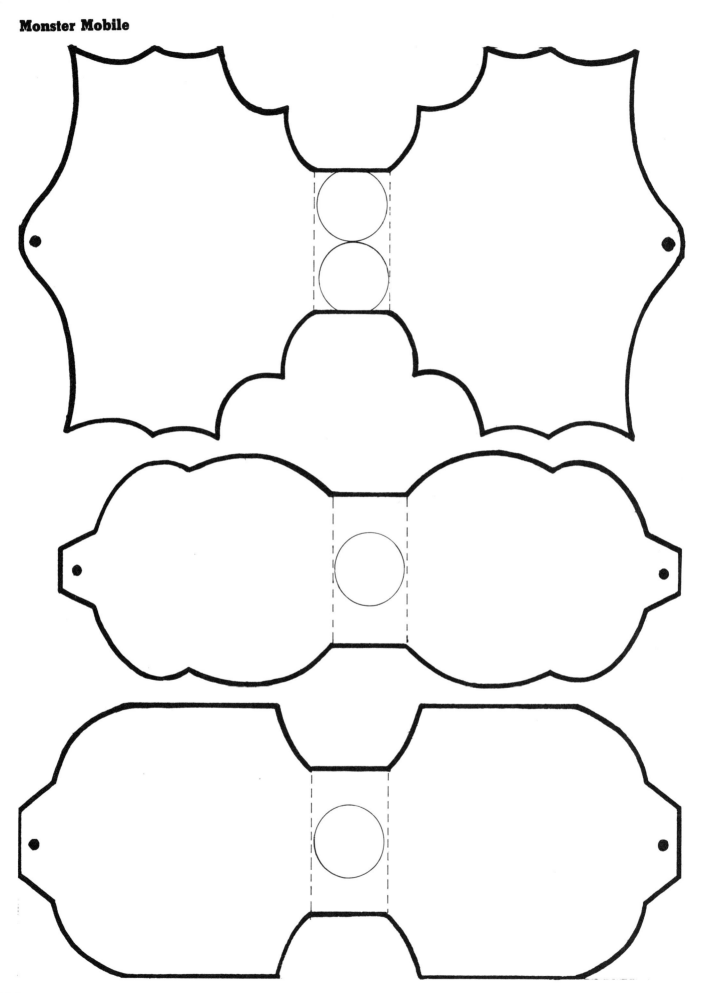

How to Make the Monster Mobile

What you will need:

12-inch ruler

pencil

string

scissors

tape

four pennies

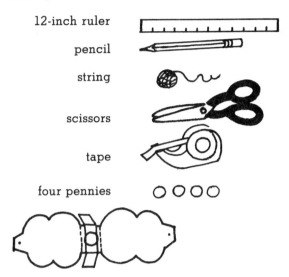

1. Cut out the three mobile monsters from the front along the solid outlines. With monsters face down, tape one penny under the Trollusk and one penny under the Yalapappus. Tape two pennies under the Bombanat. Fold the tape ends around the edges so the tape will hold securely.

fold lines

2. Fold each monster at the dotted fold lines so that the string holes meet at the top.

string holes

3. Punch through the string holes with a pencil point. Thread string through the holes and tie.

You will have three mobile monsters that look like this.

(Put a piece of tape over the strings to keep them from sliding along the pencil.)

4. Tie Trollusk and Yalapappus to pencil as shown.

5. Tie one end of a 2-foot-long string around the ruler at the 6-inch mark. Tape the string to keep it from sliding along the ruler. This will be the string you use to hang the mobile.

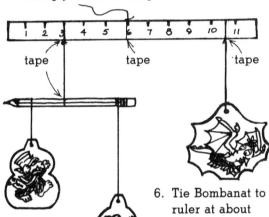

tape   tape   tape

6. Tie Bombanat to ruler at about the 10½-inch mark. Don't tape yet.

7. Tie a string around the middle of the pencil and tape it. Tie the other end of the string to the ruler at about the 3-inch mark.

8. Hang the mobile with the hanging string. If it doesn't balance, slide the side strings along the ruler until it does. Then tape them to the ruler.

Hang it up where there's a little breeze.

Monster Calendar

How to Make Your Monster Calendar

1. Tear out pages 109-120 and color the pictures.

2. Using a pencil point, punch through the three holes marked at the top of each calendar page.

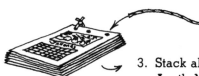

3. Stack all the pages together, with January on top, then February, March, April, May, and June. (The other months are on the backs and will be in the right order, too.) Thread strings through the two side holes and tie them in a loop. Leave the loops loose enough so you will be able to flip the pages from the front of the Monster Calendar to the back as the months change.

4. The squares on the Monster Calendar are blank because calendars change from year to year. Ask Mom or Dad to help you find a calendar for the current year so you can copy the dates into the right squares on your Monster Calendar. You don't have to wait for January to start using your Monster Calendar—begin filling in the dates in whatever month you are in now and go on from there. When you get to January on your Monster Calendar, you will be starting a new year, and you will need a calendar from the new year to copy.

5. Hang your Monster Calendar with a pushpin through the center hole. As each month ends, flip the page for that month to the back of the calendar, and the next month will be in position. When you have used all the months in one direction, just turn the whole calendar around for the rest of the months.

6. Look on page 121 for labels to cut out and paste on your calendar to mark special days.

JANUARY

SUNDAY	MONDAY	TUESDAY	WEDNESDAY	THURSDAY	FRIDAY	SATURDAY

DECEMBER

SUNDAY	MONDAY	TUESDAY	WEDNESDAY	THURSDAY	FRIDAY	SATURDAY

FEBRUARY

SUNDAY	MONDAY	TUESDAY	WEDNESDAY	THURSDAY	FRIDAY	SATURDAY

November

SUNDAY	MONDAY	TUESDAY	WEDNESDAY	THURSDAY	FRIDAY	SATURDAY

MARCH

SUNDAY	MONDAY	TUESDAY	WEDNESDAY	THURSDAY	FRIDAY	SATURDAY

OCTOBER

SUNDAY	MONDAY	TUESDAY	WEDNESDAY	THURSDAY	FRIDAY	SATURDAY

APRIL

SUNDAY	MONDAY	TUESDAY	WEDNESDAY	THURSDAY	FRIDAY	SATURDAY

SEPTEMBER

SUNDAY	MONDAY	TUESDAY	WEDNESDAY	THURSDAY	FRIDAY	SATURDAY

MAY

SUNDAY	MONDAY	TUESDAY	WEDNESDAY	THURSDAY	FRIDAY	SATURDAY

AUGUST

SUNDAY	MONDAY	TUESDAY	WEDNESDAY	THURSDAY	FRIDAY	SATURDAY

JUNE

SUNDAY	MONDAY	TUESDAY	WEDNESDAY	THURSDAY	FRIDAY	SATURDAY

JULY

SUNDAY	MONDAY	TUESDAY	WEDNESDAY	THURSDAY	FRIDAY	SATURDAY

Monster Calendar Labels for holidays and special days

Tear out the page and color the labels. Cut them out and paste them on your calendar where they belong. Some holidays (like Mother's Day and Christmas) fall on the same day or date every year—their labels are marked with the correct day or date. Other holidays (like Easter and Hanukkah) fall on a different date every year—their labels could not be marked with a day or date. Mom or Dad can help you find the right place on your calendar for them. Are there other days that are special to you? Make your own labels for them.

JANUARY 1   FEBRUARY 12   FEBRUARY 14   FEBRUARY 22   MARCH 17   APRIL 1

MOTHER'S DAY

THE SUNDAY   THE FRIDAY   SECOND SUNDAY
BEFORE EASTER   BEFORE EASTER   IN MAY

FATHER'S DAY

THIRD SUNDAY   JULY 4   FIRST MONDAY   OCTOBER 12   OCTOBER 31
IN JUNE   IN SEPTEMBER

LITTLE
MONSTER'S   EMILIA WINGBAT'S

FOURTH THURSDAY   DECEMBER 25   BIRTHDAY   CREATIVE AVIATION
IN NOVEMBER   DAY

CLEAN-UP-   LITTLE LAFF'S

MY-ROOM DAY   GIGGLE DAY

This is too much!
Every time I see you, you're
getting ready to cut something
out. Now you're probably going
to turn this page over and cut out the
MONSTER CALENDAR LABELS.
Well, go ahead—I dare you!

Walking Finger Puppets

1. Tear out the page
   and color the puppets.

2. Cut each puppet out along
   its solid outline. To cut out
   the finger holes, first punch a
   hole in each with a pencil
   point. Start cutting in the
   pencil hole and carefully cut
   around the dotted line.

3. Put your index and middle
   fingers through the finger holes
   from the back. Make the
   puppet walk by moving your
   fingers. Have a puppet on each
   hand. Make up a story for them
   to act out.

4. These
   instructions
   also work
   for the
   puppets on
   page 125.

Stamp-Collecting Trollusk

Little Monster

Paper-Munching Yalapappus

Professor Wormbog

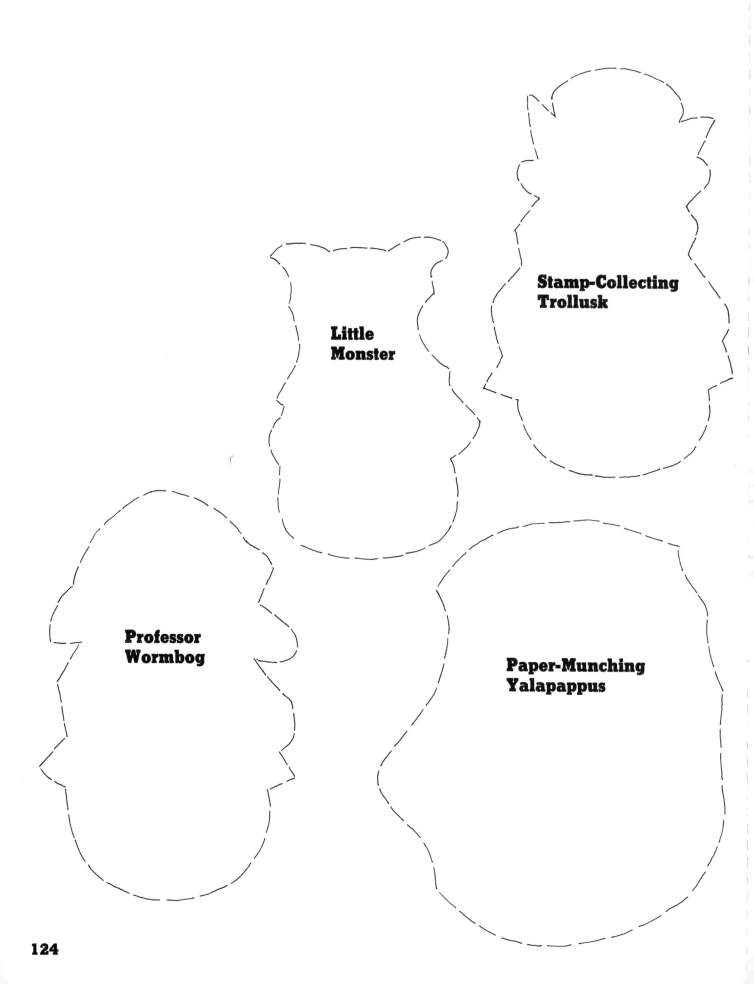

Little
Monster

Stamp-Collecting
Trollusk

Professor
Wormbog

Paper-Munching
Yalapappus

More Walking Finger Puppets

The instructions on the first page of
Walking Finger Puppets (page 123) tell
you how to make these puppets.

**Izzabella,
Queen of
Croonies**

Zipperump-a-zoo

To fasten her shoes to your
fingers, bend the tabs around
your fingers and tape.

her shoes

Little Laff

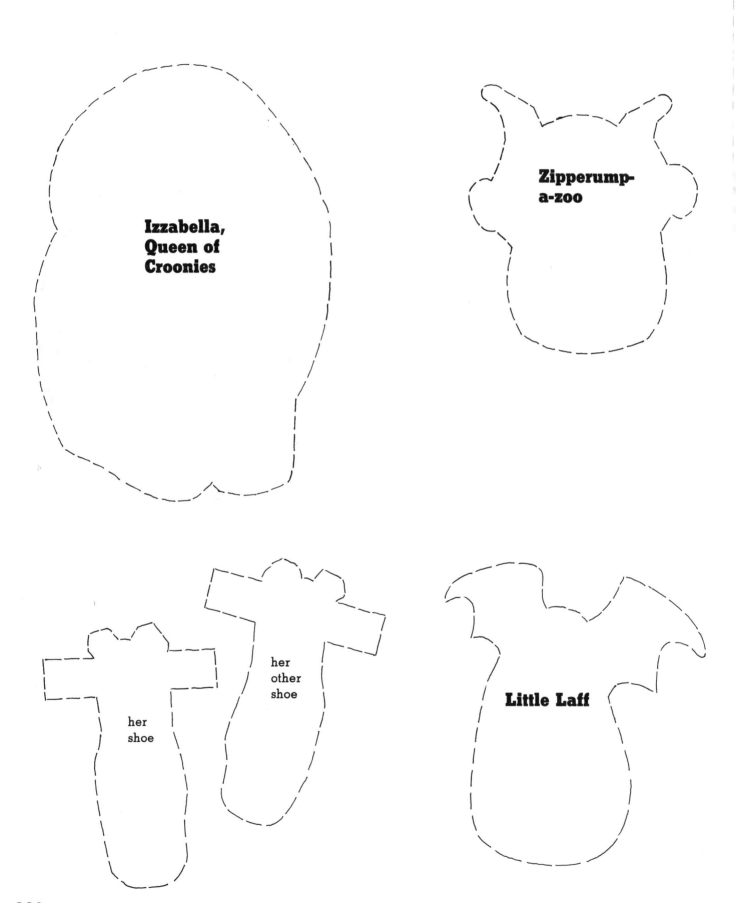

Izzabella, Queen of Croonies

Zipperump-a-zoo

her shoe

her other shoe

Little Laff

Wormbog Spinner

Can you get Professor Wormbog into the monster's mouth?

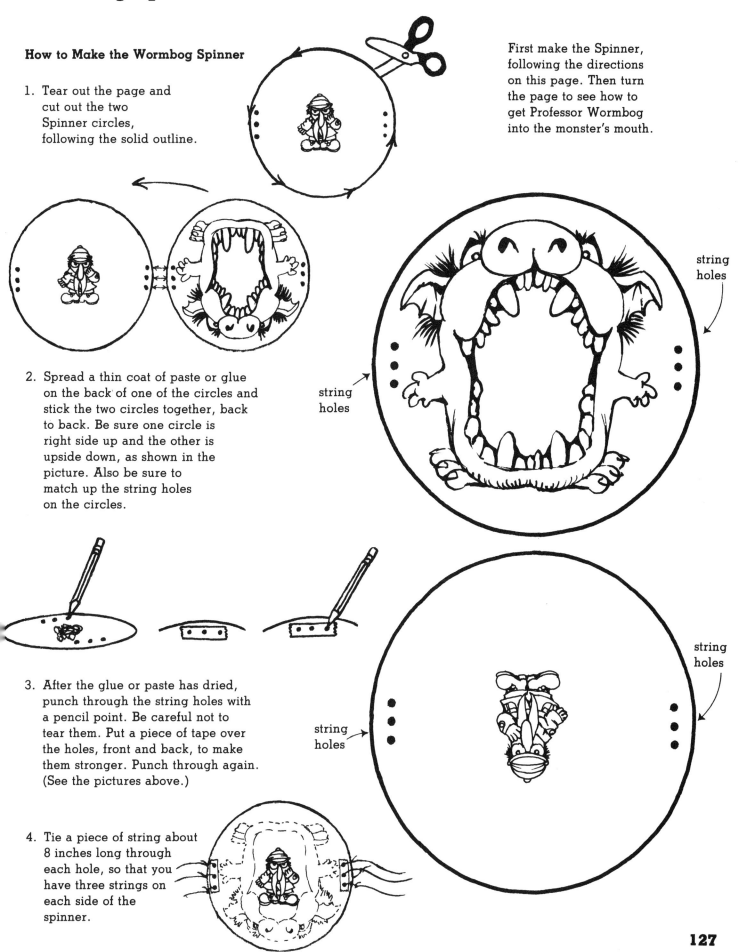

How to Make the Wormbog Spinner

1. Tear out the page and cut out the two Spinner circles, following the solid outline.

First make the Spinner, following the directions on this page. Then turn the page to see how to get Professor Wormbog into the monster's mouth.

2. Spread a thin coat of paste or glue on the back of one of the circles and stick the two circles together, back to back. Be sure one circle is right side up and the other is upside down, as shown in the picture. Also be sure to match up the string holes on the circles.

string holes

string holes

string holes

3. After the glue or paste has dried, punch through the string holes with a pencil point. Be careful not to tear them. Put a piece of tape over the holes, front and back, to make them stronger. Punch through again. (See the pictures above.)

string holes

4. Tie a piece of string about 8 inches long through each hole, so that you have three strings on each side of the spinner.

Wormbog Spinner

*Oh, what's the use—
I give up. Go ahead,
turn the page over
and cut out the
WORMBOG SPINNER
on the other side.*

*Wait a minute—I've got an idea!
I'll get a job in
another kind of book.
Hmmm. I've always
wanted to work in a
storybook. I think I'll
try it. So long, kid. You'll
have to do the rest of
this book without me.*

How to Get Professor Wormbog into the Monster's Mouth

1. Hold the ends of the strings in your hands as shown. Wind up the Spinner by twirling it around until the strings are all twisted around each other.

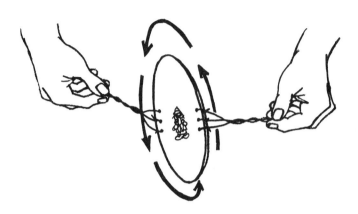

2. Make the Spinner unwind quickly by moving your hands apart, pulling the strings gently outward. Look at the spinning Spinner—Professor Wormbog will appear to be in the monster's mouth!

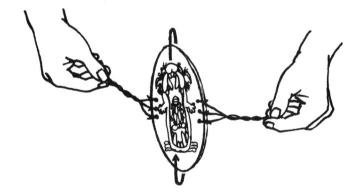

How to Draw Professor Wormbog

Follow the steps—draw lightly at first so you can erase the lines that you won't need later. He's tricky, so try again if you don't get him the first time.

1.

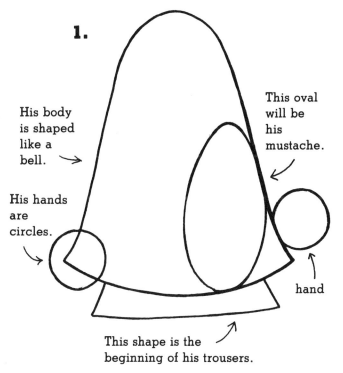

His body is shaped like a bell. →

His hands are circles. ↘

This oval will be his mustache.

hand

This shape is the beginning of his trousers.

2.

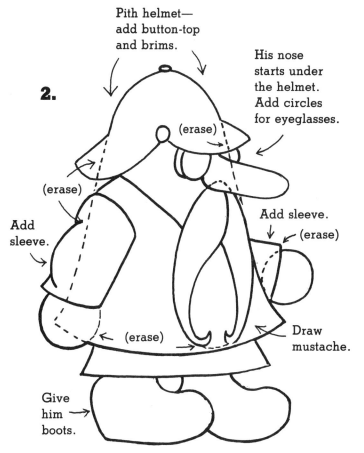

Pith helmet— add button-top and brims.

His nose starts under the helmet. Add circles for eyeglasses.

(erase)

(erase)

Add sleeve.

Add sleeve.

(erase)

Draw mustache.

Give him boots.

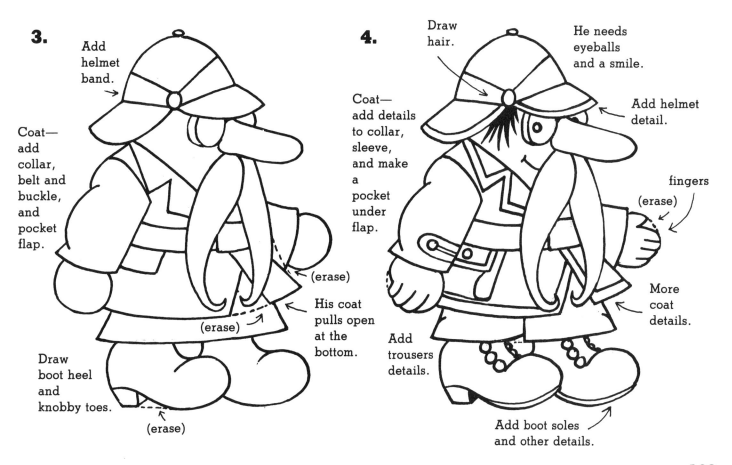

3.

Add helmet band. →

Coat— add collar, belt and buckle, and pocket flap.

(erase)

His coat pulls open at the bottom.

(erase)

Draw boot heel and knobby toes.

(erase)

4.

Draw hair.

He needs eyeballs and a smile.

Coat— add details to collar, sleeve, and make a pocket under flap.

Add helmet detail.

fingers

(erase)

More coat details.

Add trousers details.

Add boot soles and other details.

More Paper-Bag Puppets

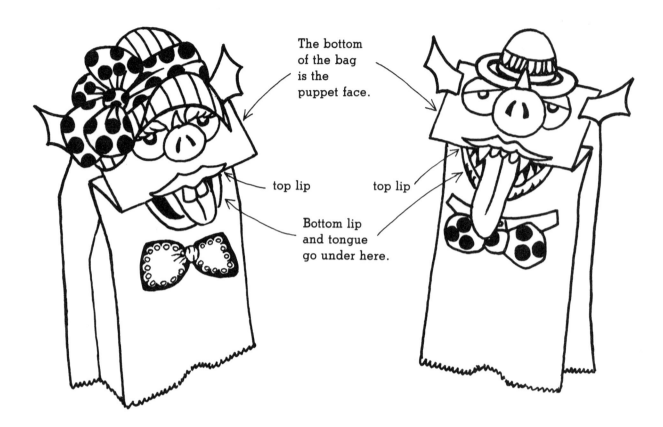

The bottom of the bag is the puppet face.

top lip

top lip

Bottom lip and tongue go under here.

How to Make Them

1. You will need two small paper bags, one for each puppet.

2. Tear out page 131 and color the puppet pieces. Cut out the pieces around the solid outlines.

3. The bottom of the paper bag is the puppet face. Choose eyes, ears, snout, and hat for each puppet and paste or tape them to a bag bottom. You can use the pictures above for a guide, or design your own faces.

4. Choose a top lip for each puppet and paste or tape it to the edge of the bag bottom.

5. a. For one puppet, the bottom mouth-part and tongue are already together.
   b. To make the bottom mouth-part for the other puppet, tape the tongue onto the bottom mouth-part as shown.

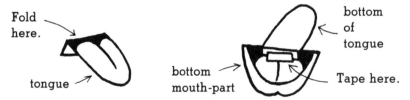

Fold here.

tongue

bottom mouth-part

bottom of tongue

Tape here.

6. Tape the bottom mouth-part of each puppet under the edge of the bag bottom. Line it up with the top lip.

7. Give one puppet the collar and bow tie, and give the other the lacy bow.

More Paper-Bag Puppets—Puppet Pieces

bow

upper lip

hat

upper lip

snout

eye

collar

ears

ear

tongue

eye

bottom mouth-part

eye

bottom mouth-part

bow tie

hat

ear

eye

snout

upper
lip

bow

hat

upper
lip

eye

snout

ear

ear

collar

ear

bottom
mouth-part

eye

bottom
mouth-part

tongue

eye

bow
tie

hat

snout

eye

ear

Window on the Edge of Nowhere—Day

Hang this window on your wall and you'll be looking out at the Edge of Nowhere where all the Monsters live. When night comes, turn your window over, and you'll be looking out at a nighttime scene. Turn the page to see how to get your window ready to hang.

Window on the Edge of Nowhere—Night

Tear out this page and color both sides. Cut out the window. Punch through the hole marked at the top of the window with a pencil point. Put a piece of sticky tape over the hole and punch through again. Tie a piece of string through the hole. Use the string to hang your window on the wall. Now you can turn your window to either side, for day or night.

It's a Blowfat-Glowfish!

Color this picture and hang it on your wall.

You-Can-Make-It Monster Greeting Cards

The next eight pages have greeting cards you can cut out, color, and send to your friends. There are two cards each for birthdays, Valentine's Day, Halloween, and Christmas.

To Make a Greeting Card:

1. Choose the card that you want to send and tear out the page it's on. Color the card and cut it out along the solid outline.

2. Fold the card in half lengthwise, so that the picture is on the front and the greeting is on the inside.

3. Sign your name, put the card in an envelope, and address the envelope. Don't forget to put a stamp on it. You might put some Trollusk Stamps on it, too—they are on page 37 of this book.

Surprise a friend—
send a Monster Greeting Card today!

A Monster Card
by Mercer Mayer
from
Little Monster's
You-Can-Make-It Book

A Monster Card
by Mercer Mayer
from
Little Monster's
You-Can-Make-It Book

Happy Birthday

Be sure to blow out the candles before you eat the cake!

from_____

Here's a cute
little pet for
your birthday.

from_____

A Monster Card
by Mercer Mayer
from
Little Monster's
You-Can-Make-It Book

BE MY VALENTINE

A Monster Card
by Mercer Mayer
from
Little Monster's
You-Can-Make-It Book

May you have
Izzabella,
Queen of Croonies
for your
VALENTINE!

from_____

Valentine,
I'm eating
my heart out
over you.

from_____

A Monster Card
by Mercer Mayer
from
Little Monster's
You-Can-Make-It Book

A Monster Card
by Mercer Mayer
from
Little Monster's
You-Can-Make-It Book

BOO!

Have a
scarey
Halloween.

from_____

It's
Halloween,
so
Bats to You!

from
Bat-Hilda
and

_____

A Monster Card
by Mercer Mayer
from
Little Monster's
You-Can-Make-It Book

A Monster Card
by Mercer Mayer
from
Little Monster's
You-Can-Make-It Book

143

**Merry
Zipperump-a-zoo
and
Christmas, too!**

from_____

**Merry
Christmas**

Hope you get
everything
you asked for.

from_____